Passages

Passages

Hollyhocks on
the Garden Wall

Louise Netherton

Passages: Hollyhocks on the Garden Wall

Published by Wheatmark®
610 East Delano Street, Suite 104
Tucson, Arizona 85705 U.S.A.
www.wheatmark.com

International Standard Book Number: 978-1-60494-111-1
Library of Congress Control Number: 2008925330

Journey of Grief

Passages: *Hollyhocks on the Garden Wall* is a narrative of my emotional journey as a widow. I was married almost fifty-seven years when, after a long battle with cancer, my husband lost the battle.

There was a positive blessing at the end because of hospice. The last three weeks he was pain free, was alert, and enjoyed family and friends. Our great granddaughter, four years old, was a delight for him. They enjoyed a Frosty every afternoon, and in the morning she waited patiently for her grandpa to get up and help her pick a grapefruit for breakfast.

Ned had a sense of humor. Our daughter told me he played an April Fools' joke on her. Six days later he passed away.

Two years have passed and I continue to reconstruct my life. I was encouraged to write a journal, and to my surprise emotions and tears flowed into words. The journal does not have closure. In the experience of losing my husband a part of me died. My grief will always be with me. Still, I continue to rebuild my life.

In sharing my experience of loss, I hope it may have some value to others who are grieving.

This journal is dedicated to my dear husband, Ned; our daughters and their husbands, Barbara and Dennis, Jo Ellen and Charlie, and Peggy; grandchildren; great grandchildren, especially little Billie; and to our extended families in the

States and abroad. Last of all it is dedicated to our circle of friends who gave me love, support, and strength.

With Ned's words "We'll get through this, Louise," I continue each day knowing he was confident I would survive.

Passages

Grief Counseling

Because of grief counseling I kept a journal. It is not a journal of what I did or did not do each day, but a journal of my thoughts after losing the one I loved.

I share this journal in the hope that it helps you understand what took place in my thoughts. For each individual the loss is different; all have unresolved problems, and all suffer the pain of losing a loved one. The floodgates of death release the barriers that protect us from life's conflicts.

All of us are victims of death. If it was our husband or wife whom we were fortunate to have by our sides "in sickness and health," "till death do us part," we did not think about "till death do us part" until reality confronted us. Suddenly we had no choice.

Through the months I have become sensitive to others who have lost a loved one. I have now walked in their shoes, having experienced the pain they are facing. I realize the deep loss, the lonely nights we all face.

To say "death is a part of life" does nothing to ease the reality, coming home to a house, no one there to come home to, having experiences but no one to share them with. An empty chair at the table, the empty side of the bed, everywhere— empty. No razor on his side of the sink (or cosmetics on her side), the empty hole in your heart.

I am fortunate. I am blessed with good health, a renewed

teaching certificate, and the opportunity to fill the empty days.

I still am not sure that alone will get me through this year of my life. I am trying. I am thankful for my family, friends, and caring others who have given of their love and time to support me throughout this year. I try to listen, to understand and accept help, but it is my responsibility to choose life or death, to choose to continue alone or to give up. Whatever I choose in the future is my responsibility.

I didn't realize how much I loved you till you were no longer at my side.

We shared our lives. We shared our thoughts, our dreams, our successes and our failures. We shared our bed, our love of living. We shared our family, extending the concept of family across the world. We shared our love of music, the arts, and travel. We shared our laughter and our tears.

Now it's good-bye. Too soon. We had no choice.

I place a rose on your place in the earth. It will die and mingle with the desert dust. Dearest, can you know how much I miss you?

Memory—dust

Memory fades—dust blows away.

Memory—you can't touch it, feel it, or even experience it. You can't enfold it in your arms.

We're physical biological beings. So are all other living creatures on Earth.

What is memory? An evolutionary solution for survival? A process evolving within every living organism to ensure its adaptation in a changing environment? As humans at the apex of evolution, memory becomes not only a tool for survival, but an insurance policy that enables us to come to terms with life's realities.

Is memory a photograph? I want to photograph the sparkle, the love of life in your eyes. I want to hear the sound of your voice, and to again experience the warmth of your body next to mine. I want to photograph the sound of your footsteps coming in the room. I want to hear your voice in your time of need.

I will try to live for the future. You wanted that. "Louise, we'll get through this."

I am afraid my memory will fade away as the dust blows.

Grief and loss are different for each survivor. Possibly the answer is that death opens the floodgates and all of the complex unresolved demons of the past come rushing in. The safety net of love, stability, companionship, and future is swept away in floods of emotions. The life jackets of family, faith, strength, and support of those who care keep survivors afloat.

Death leaves some naked, sweeping away all other defenses that were built through the years.

I find myself vulnerable to the silence, no longer having my love beside me. All of our years together, his encouragement, strength, and stability were there for me. His first gift to me were oil paints, because he learned I liked to draw. Later in life he was my best promoter and critic. We used to laugh, if he didn't like a painting I usually sold it.

Now I would sell my soul just to hear him say "Louise, did you read the speed limit?" "Did you forget anything on the table?" (I often forgot the napkins or something else.) "Keep your voice down," when I got carried away. When I had a stupid car accident (we had secrets—we didn't want the kids to be upset) he should have chewed me out; instead he picked me up and said, "Where should we take it for repairs?" I wish I could hear him call "Louise" in the night when he needed help. He was so grateful for whatever I did for him.

In one of our private moments of agony he said, "Louise,

we'll get through this." Those words have given me so much comfort—just knowing he was confident of my ability to carry on.

Yet so many times that confidence falters. The floodgates are open and I am faced with unresolved, buried-childhood-past, before-marriage emotions. I did not have the stability of parents, ancestors. Growing up in rural America in the 30s there were no school counselors for kids or parents. These are not excuses, but there are many ghosts that come back now that the floodgates are open.

I am trying to move on knowing it is up to me. Unlike in my youth, there is a reason to live. We have three wonderful daughters, six grandchildren, and a great grandson and granddaughter. In the last days our great granddaughter in her short life (four years) brought joy to her great grandfather. In the morning she patiently waited for him to get up and they would pick their grapefruit for breakfast. Barbara took a photo of this activity, for which I am thankful. In the afternoon they shared a frozen yogurt together. I hope I never desert them.

Every day is a battle to face a new day. I miss my husband more than I ever realized I would. I cry for him and for me. The curtain of death is so final. Some people find a hole in that curtain. I beg for that hole—we even had a secret password between us.

No avail, not even a dream. No feeling he is by my side, no faith. I envy those whose faith sustain them. I have no comfort in what I don't experience or understand. There are no prayers or wailing wall, or beads, or prayer papers to burn or meditation to sustain me.

I appreciate all the love and support of family and friends, but I know the responsibility is mine as to what to do in the future. I need help to make the right decisions.

It's the third day—empty day. Half blurred in sleep—in dreams out of focus—mere brain waves that register activity somewhere in the depths of despair.

Yes, part of the day was retrieved. I made some cookies to share with friends. I wrote several letters, a couple to inform past friends of my loss. I did not want to wait till the holidays to inform of death. A greeting card is to give love and directional lights for the New Year.

Grief counseling, many activities, homework, exercises meant to help erase an event, no, not erase, but push it in the shadows to be resurrected on future occasions. Perhaps more to help one manage the waves, out-of-control emotions that a loved one's loss brings. Writing letters to a loved one, the intention is to voice unfinished communications cut short by death. I cannot write to ashes buried in the earth. I wrote my last love letter and laid it softly in the beautiful little box with you till eternity. Now I write to myself pouring out my anguish, my pain, my soul spilling out on paper like an inkblot that stains the soul.

I am not sure of soul. I am sure there is a knife pain in deep belly that boils up within. Violent, producing salty tears and crying for relief. At times it sneaks up like a thief in the night seeking to subdue a victim. All reason is distorted, drowning in self-pity, loss of control, and loss of confidence.

Tonight is another night. Tomorrow is another day, then another and another. Will they always be the same?

I am a widow.

Is it possible the word is willow? Weeping branches sweeping earth and sighing in the storm-tossed night.

No, it is widow.

One night death stole away my love, my life, my heart; its icy breath made me a widow.

Being a widow defines who I am, what I do, and my place in society. In ancient cultures widows joined death on the funeral fire. Suddenly being a widow demands an instant adjustment in society. Amid the mourning it is necessary not to drown in self-pity.

Maybe it's a time to rehearse for a new role in life in which the widow plays the starring role. She will also write the play. The play will tell of lonely unfulfilled nights where a new dawn comes too soon. Another day to walk alone, to be the keeper of the keys. Another challenge is what role the widow plays in our culture, her relationships in the past and in the future. The role can intrude on those whose lives were entwined with the widow in the past.

Thinking again of the willow—it is important to stand alone as the willow tree and the tears will wash away the debris. I remember as a child the willow trees grew along the river-banks. It is easy to imagine they truly wept tears and they would flow from the river to the sea.

The new role is difficult and different for every widow. The role is interpreted in many ways. The role can be played with dignity, hope, life, or as an empty ghost on life's stage. Some will see this play and be moved and uplifted, or they will feel it is a boring drama, a broken record they have heard before.

A widow's lines aren't written for her. She will have to ad-lib each act. The first act is an empty stage—with crying in the night, and questions for truth. The second act is a personal interpretation. Will this act address some of the unanswered questions, the search and pursuit for meaning in life? The third act is either a victory when the curtain goes down, or the act ends in submission to the dark forces that were born in the first act. Dark forces that stole the identity of the character.

I am a widow. I have to interpret my new role. I have to write my own script. I will develop the character. My character will either overcome the dark forces or be subdued by inner fears and self-pity. At this writing I am only in the first act. Still the questions come, the time of mourning has not passed. I do not know when I will begin to write the next act.

It rained tonight, wonderful refreshing rain. I fixed a salad to eat on the patio. It's only 6:30—now what?

For some reason I began thinking of an experience in Uruguay, probably because the wind blew so furiously for a bit. I remember at our apartment complex a little penguin was blown in one night from the southern Falkland Islands. It had been blown north off course, alone with probably no hope of survival.

Somehow I feel like that little penguin, blown off course without hope of survival. I have no idea why this incident came to me after about twenty-five years. It's one of the images of despair that seem to stimulate me more often. I know I should have positive thoughts. I wonder if we have control of where our thoughts may lead us.

As usual the evening is spread before me. I have a book, TV, computer, and I have me. I am not comfortable with me. I am not comfortable with my thoughts. I am afraid of myself.

I remember the last night Ned was in hospice. I don't think I gave him a hug or final kiss—no good-bye. I left it up to the nurses to tend to his needs; then he was sleeping peacefully (I thought) and I wanted to be with him. That is why I stayed. Yet in the final hour I deserted him—I should have woken him up—I should have been there. I left the room. When I returned, he was gone. I should have been more aware. I did not say good-bye.

I'm on the patio looking through the neighbor's small tree.

It's almost dark but through the holes I see the sky. To me they represent holes in a tapestry—the tapestry that we both wove of our lives with loving care. It was a tapestry filled with exciting events, with children, with sharing the complexities of life and dreams fulfilled. Now death has ripped holes in that tapestry. It cannot be repaired.

It will be stored away in my heart, reminding me of a gentle, caring soul who dedicated his life to me. He gave me his name, his love and support, encouragement to become the person I am today. He encouraged me to be capable, responsible, creative, and independent. He was truly my friend and soul mate.

Yet he would be dismayed at the deep dark thoughts that take over my loneliness. I fight an inward battle to continue to be the person he would be proud of and our girls would be proud of. I need to find a focus, a purpose in life, a reason to get up in the morning. I fear the months ahead.

It's been three months today when I lost Ned. I had to go to the mortuary to refuse a plaque that was incorrect. I did a small painting. I tried to get air tickets to go to our daughters for Thanksgiving—without success. I'll try another day.

I kept busy; in-between I touched your clothes. I looked in your billfold (I never did this in your life—it was your private space) but I wanted to touch what you had touched. I wanted so much to feel you near me.

I attend the grief sessions at the church. I promised our daughters I would do this. It gives them comfort to know I am trying to get through this. They all live in other states.

I hope the grief counseling will ward off depression. There are still all of your medications in your closet. I would like to join you, but need the courage to die or to live. Am not sure which to do.

You would be proud of me so far, of how I am handling the everyday mundane problems, big and little. Resetting the clocks, selling the van, caring for the plants (though I am not the gardener you were—I kill some) putting salt in the water softener, etc. I am learning but depression still stalks me. It is so difficult to imagine the months and years ahead without you. Empty, empty, a deep dark hole!

I wrote this poem to give at a presentation of the artist Christo's exhibit of umbrellas on the hills of California. Ned and I were so fortunate to be in the area during the exhibit. Seeing this exhibit in the early morning light, the umbrellas dancing across the hills, was so exciting. To me it was a fusion of natural beauty giving a backdrop to man's creativity.

Now I am free, suddenly the poem I wrote has lost wind, like a balloon that has lost air.

I am free—from what? Loving, responsibility, schedules, seeing meals are on the table, laundry done, chasing a spider from its secret hiding place, etc. This new freedom is not what I envisioned when I wrote the poem. My new freedom means walking through life alone.

Let me be free
May the colors wrap me in a mantle
Sweep me up in swirling winds of
Enthusiasm to soar breathlessly
A moment in time.

Let me be free
To play with form and mold my dreams
Into reality,
For just a moment.

Let me be free
To experience, to share with all

Of you who have dared to dream
With me
For just a moment.

Again—writing, I guess it is a way of healing, a journal, but I am not sure.

I had a busy day. I checked in at school, visited a friend, wrapped a gift for a child, etc. In spite of all of the activity the tears have come more frequent without outside stimulation.

Last night a little frog jumped in our water fountain. I discovered him and was so excited; then I realized I had no one to share the fun news with. Tonight there he was again. A little creature friend—if only I could tell him how welcome he is. The same, if only I could share with Ned our little frog, the beautiful flowers on the patio, the sunset on the mountains, and on and on.

Living in a retirement community has its plus and minus. At night I feel so isolated. I miss the sounds, smells, bright lights, children's voices, just signs of being alive.

At this time I cannot share these doubts, or pain, with our daughters. They are far away (and that is good as they have their lives, families) and I would never want them to worry. It is true I am fine! Someday I will share these thoughts with them as it may help them to understand my pain in losing a husband. They too have experienced the pain of losing their father. The process?

I am proud that so far I have found strength to "overcome," but only with the caring and love of people who have walked the extra mile with me. I have been given the insight to face the future, and temporary shoulders to lean on. I am so fortunate.

I mark this date in my mind. I used to mark dates on the calendar, wedding dates, due dates, graduation dates, airline dates, birthdays, etc. Now this date looks backward. It has been four months since I said good-bye forever to my soul mate.

I went early to the cemetery to leave a rose (from one Ned had planted). I suspect the good it does is to give me a feeling of caring. By the way, the flag next to our plot is a rag. Tatters. The next time I go I will replace it with a new flag. Ned's name is washed away on the temporary paper sign that identified his space there. I cannot understand why this mortuary is so inefficient.

This afternoon I drove into Tucson (alone) for a movie, *Akeelah and the Bee.* Wonderful story of a child from the ghetto who succeeded, but with the help of others.

I can relate. I truly believe many children can be saved if they have an adult who can intervene in early years.

I have a friend who attended a meditation meeting. I realize that help is not one size fits all. For me meditation would be so painful I am sure I would commit suicide if I had to face myself.

At the end of the day I've run out of water for tears. Every day I am trying to refocus my life, but I don't know where.

When will I stop writing?

Tonight is a calm evening. Rain showers marched down the valley near the mountains. I took photos of our bird-of-paradise against the dark skies.

I am enjoying this August evening, the soft evening light on the mountains, the sound of our water fountain, etc. It is so bittersweet to sit here alone enjoying, feeling so safe in our home. Ned moved because of his love for me. He loved his former garden that was beautiful. We both agreed we were at the time of life when neither of us could take care of the garden.

Yet I sit here, I pretend he'll join me in a minute, then we'll sit together, and have an evening visit. In the last months we had so much to talk about, an exchange of thoughts and concerns, and decisions to be made. Yet the reality of losing my mate was too much for me to acknowledge. I was in denial. I refused to let my thoughts enter that realm of dark reality.

Now I try to adjust to the quiet evening alone, depending on the second rum and coke to help me get through the next few hours till I can drift into sleep wishing to dream, but I don't dream, don't connect, realizing that my loss is forever.

Today our daughter flew back to her home in California. We had a terrific four days together. Besides shopping we saw a movie, went to see the musical *The Lion King*, and attended the concert in Reed Park on Sunday night. We had time for sharing, laughter, and fun. It is such a blessing to have all of our daughters.

In the evening I planted some pots with new flowers. But by 7 PM depression begin to set in, the lonely lost feeling. Seems like all of the weeks of healing progress have disappeared. I want to cry and cry—am I wallowing in self-pity, or true grief?

Common sense tells me I would not have wanted Ned to suffer through another summer. But if I could only reach out one more time—just to touch him, hear his voice, and share with him our daughter's visit. Reality is so painful.

I thought I was past the pain, but not tonight. It almost seems like the night I lost him. Another coming home and no one to come home to. I feel like a dam broke—all of the depression, tears, and pain tend to envelop me.

Next week would have been his eighty-eighth birthday. Yet I am so thankful he had such a full, wonderful life.

I will miss buying him a birthday present, no wrapping it, no candles to light, no party.

I will take a rose to the cemetery. I think of all the years we have gone to the cemetery remembering our loved ones, but I never envisioned myself visiting my loved one there.

This summer I have made a lot of progress. I gave away my option to choose death, now I have to tough it out. I have such a wonderful family (don't live close) and friends who support me, so it's up to me not to disappoint them.

The last three days have been difficult. Three days ago one of our dearest friends passed away. It was the second heart operation by the most skilled doctor in the state.

That night I woke up crying—thought I couldn't stop. I kept thinking I am past this. Then the next morning I learned the sad news about Marge. Coincidence—I don't know.

Yesterday I planted a tree in our yard. It is a lovely crepe myrtle tree. I dug the hole with the help of our neighbor, who loaned me his miner's pick. That worked great until I punched a hole in the water line! My neighbor said, "Louise, I thought you wanted to take an outdoor shower!" Better laugh than cry. The plumber came right out and fixed the line. I finished digging the hole. When the tree was delivered the man just popped it in the hole. Easy for me. This morning I tidied up the mess, removed the excess soil, and was so pleased.

As the day progressed I relapsed. I felt such a deep depression—I planted the tree in Ned's memory. I should be happy. I realized he will never see its beautiful bloom. Last spring there were three trees planted at Continental School in memory of Ned for the work he did with the children's gardening project.

His birthday is next week. The tree is his present—I also bought a memorial box for the flag that was presented to me at the time of his death. This container for the flag is also a gift from our daughters. Memorials—memories—suddenly I am not sure I can endure the pain, and the pride in my heart for my husband.

October 6 it will be six months. I've made so much progress this summer—just adjusting to being a widow, and trying to live a "normal" life. Life is not the same, not normal.

I was at the desk at Tubac Arts today. So many happy couples visited the Arts Center. One couple was from England, another from an eastern state. I greeted them and tried to make them feel welcome. Yet there was a nagging pain in my heart. In past years when I volunteered in Tubac, Ned would meet me and we would go to the Cow Palace for dinner. Always my thoughts turn to Ned. I knew when I drove home he wouldn't be here.

The pain goes on—I have regressed.

Ned's nephew and niece are coming tomorrow. I look forward to their visit. We'll do fun things. Ned's family is my family. I hope they are not disappointed in their first visit. I hope I will be in control of my emotions. They are young and happy. I don't want them to feel the shadow of my pain. For that matter I want to get past the pain too and move on.

It's September—holidays are coming. I will need help to get through these holidays.

Cemetery

Quiet
Quiet
Blue skies
Lazy clouds
Sun giving light
Tree giving relief from sun.

Quiet
Frightening
Soul crying out
Quiet, hearing my own heart beat
Quiet, confronting dark thoughts.
Quiet, feel the pain
Quiet, hear the pain
Soul reaching out for answers
Soul needing release from pain.

Quiet, fantasy wishes.
Take me home
Take me to somewhere place
Somewhere place
I'll touch my love.

Why is the barrier so impenetrable?
A wall that cannot be scaled
A veil separating the living and the dead.
Cries of the Universe
Cannot be heard,
Trapped souls on both sides
Trapped in eternal ages.

Last night I dreamed of Ned.

All these months I begged through tears just to connect in my dreams. I subconsciously thought it would bring peace, closing, good-bye.

In the dream he was in a large room and as usual I can't remember details, but I was outside this room with several people. Somehow a trip was being discussed (not sure what kind, camping or road) and I decided to go inside and ask Ned if he felt we should go on this trip. I started to open the glass door but the door stuck; he got up and came to open the door, but then it did open. He went back to his chair and looked so well. Somehow in the dream I was aware he had passed away, but now he was OK. He was wearing a plain blue shirt, and light beige trousers. He looked so nice as always with his beautiful white hair. I thought all of the other was a dream and he was really with me. I bent over to kiss him and it must have been like putting out a candle. I was awake—I sat up and found myself shaking. There was no embrace—no touching him—no hello or good-bye.

I had wanted to embrace him, then I realized it was like the last night. Depression gripped me. The reality of the last night of his life—he was gone and I did not embrace, I did not say good-bye. I failed. Even in my dream I was not able to bring closure. I did not erase the guilt. I did not find the peace I imagined.

I took my walk—I took a shower—I returned to normalcy—

I put on the coffee and on the refrigerator was his photo. The same blue shirt and beige trousers, the last event he attended with me—a reception at Hilltop Gallery. Now only a photo, only a memory. The pain of loss is still so fresh. Seven months.

Reality

No more sunrise
No more sunsets
No more walks around the block
No more hikes
No more wildflowers
No more music
Waterfalls
Birds
Wind
Footsteps
Children's voices
Laughter
Tears
Pain
It's over!

Darkness
Nonexistence
Ashes
In a box
Faded rose on top
Tears mixed with earth
A name carved in stone.

Who will remember?
Generations to come
Will not know that name.
Maybe they will know
Real people existed
Who lived,

Loved
Walked upon this earth
And gave love
To those they left behind.

Evenings are for remembering the day. It's the time of sharing, the time to usher in the night. Nocturnal life walks softly upon the earth. There is a mystery, a romantic coupling of life. The dance, the music plays on, promising to bring a new day.

Yet for some of us it is the evening of our lives. Death quietly arrives having stalked its victim. For the loved ones who are left the evening no longer promises the dance of life. Instead the memories to be shared are ghosts of the past, hard, cold, fleeting reminders of life.

Being left behind, there is a struggle to exist, each night there seems to be an undercurrent that threatens to sweep the soul out to sea.

Happiness

Is being in tune with life.
The sights and sounds of the living,
Laughter, quiet whispers,
Tree branches singing in the wind,
Raindrops on skylights.
Frog jumping in pond,
The music of living
Is what defines happiness.

But sometimes when the heart is empty
The soul has fled.
Happiness falls on deaf ears.
Happiness is an echo of the past
No longer brings peace,
No longer defined.
Happiness is like a thin jacket,
No longer warm and fuzzy,
Too thin to protect against icy realities.

Happiness becomes a place
Wherein we try to hide our pain.

Life has come full circle.

My childhood was lonely. I had no heritage, no relatives or friends. But happy. I chased butterflies, picked wild strawberries, watched mother muskrat quietly float on the lazy stream with her little ones following behind, and found a fragile luna moth on a wet morning leaf. I had a wonderful playmate who never left my side. She secretly ran races with me, shared my stories however outrageous they were, and helped me wish upon a star and dream of faraway places.

Then suddenly she was gone—like "Puff the Magic Dragon," never to return again.

The real world brought adjustments; the largest was how to relate to real people. Through education and kind teachers I was able to prepare for the future.

Then a real friend who would become my soul mate came into my life.

The years passed so quickly—love, family, dreams fulfilled were life's gifts for me. We mastered the secrets of love, not only for each other but enough left over for others whose lives crossed ours. Together we explored the world, and embraced the rich cultures that gave us an appreciation of others' beliefs and customs. Our world was rich and beautiful.

All of this part of our life ended. Now when I walk it is only my shadow upon the earth. There is no one beside me to love.

Life has come full circle for me. Now again I talk to the invisible. I hold his billfold close to my heart, I touch his glasses, I wear his wedding ring on a chain, I listen to myself pour out my thoughts, my pain to silence. I walk alone. Life's memories are ghosts reminding me of all I've lost.

Yet I am thankful to have had love to embrace, if now only in my heart.

Today is November 6—it marks the seventh month I have walked alone. The pain of loss is still so raw.

This is about me. I realize how selfish I am. I think about the word mourning—am I mourning my dearest soul mate, or am I mourning the loss of part of me?

Today I went to the cemetery especially to check to see if the flag was OK. Tomorrow is Veteran's Day.

Ashes in a box. I am there remembering his soft smile, his beautiful white hair, the loving, caring life he gave me, the twinkle in his eye. Now I am glad his ashes aren't on the mountaintop (he once thought that would be a good idea) so I can come to this sacred place to lay a rose. I want so much to feel his presence. I want to think that maybe, just maybe he knows I come. Maybe he knows how much I love and miss him.

Nothing, just heartbroken feelings. I have lost so much. Yet our daughter is with me today, she is the product of our love, she is our future, she and her sisters are the reason to live, to make them proud of me.

I pull myself together and get on with the day. Grocery shopping, luncheon with artist friends and a lousy movie.

Now it is evening. Alone time. Barb and her husband went to a movie, they asked me, but I had my movie for the day, and I believe it is important for them to have their time together.

I feel so selfish. Others have not had so many years together, and some widows tell me it's been two, five, or ten years they have been alone. It has been seven months and I can't imagine how they got through those years. I do well to get from one morning to the next and get through the day.

Yes, this is about me. How will I face the challenges ahead? Some days I don't even know myself. I pretend to be happy, to be confident, but it is so easy to get sidetracked, lose the rational train of thought, and my mind wanders into forbidden territory. Every morning I face a new day alone. I never realized how special it was just to prepare hot oatmeal with nuts, and a banana for my loved one.

Veterans Day

I remembered the flag. It waves for him. I force myself not to cry. I'm proud I remembered how much it meant to Ned to fly the flag on special days. For you, my darling, I remembered.

I wanted to cry on someone's shoulder. Our daughter is here but I don't want her to begin the morning with my tears. I know a dear friend ... "No, Louise, that is not fair—don't touch the phone!" I've made progress. It's easier to face my loss alone. The time has passed when I can use my family and friends as a crutch to keep me going. Now seven months, how many more? I have to survive the future one morning at a time.

Today I was a greeter at the Tubac Arts. So many happy people pass through. Sometimes a couple visits the gallery enjoying the exhibit and each other. I unexpected get a knot in my stomach and fight back the tears. My mind flashes back to the years Ned and I enjoyed travel, exhibits, theater, and friends together.

It's a challenge to have an interest in tomorrow when part of my life has been shattered, I need to pick up the pieces, be responsible, and have the courage to move ahead. I owe this to our terrific daughters whom I love dearly.

In My Daughter's Home/California

Thanksgiving

Moments, hours,
Happiness filled the house.
Beauty in preparations,
Sounds, chopping,
Timers, clang of pans,
Aromas, laughter
And trips to the
Grocery store.

On this one spot
On Earth everything gave thanks.
Even a small blossom
On the Camellia bush
Appeared one last time
To thank the world
Before winter's nap.

Drink it in slowly
Like wine.
Hold the moment
As long as possible.
Champagne
One last toast to life
Searching for the sea.

It seemed like a dream.
I was already dead.
Listening to voices,

Laughter of the future,
Looking, feeling,
Pride swelling in my heart,
My family.

How confident the future in their hands,
The agony of the world continues—
But they are strong.
Generations to come will someday make things
Right in this turbulent world.

I am thankful I was given these gifts to hold
A short time in my walk on earth,

The Camellia bush had one last gift to give—
In early morning sunlight, a large, fragile,
Beautifully constructed spiderweb
Tied to slender branches
Swings softly in space,
A miracle so magical exists
in this moment,
nature's gift
Of beauty and order on Earth,
And healing for my broken heart.

On Monday night I listened to part of the music from South Pacific on public TV. I thought about my day.

I drove to Tucson to complete gift shopping. First I bought a golf shirt for Dennis—walking into the men's department was difficult.

I thought about all the fun shirts I used to buy for Ned. When the day ended I was over budget—same as every year. But fun to try and guess how to surprise and please my loved ones.

At the end of the day I felt like a yo-yo, up and down. The down part was the absence of my husband. Amid self-pity, tears, and a deep sense of fear, not sure of the future, failure, not understanding myself, probably loss of control, and the realization amid all of the holiday celebrations my heart does not respond. Loss of faith is not new—it always has been a lifelong-searching-swinging-between-believing, non-believing/commitment or failure. Now when I want so much to hope, to believe, I am drained, lost, facing the future empty of faith, walking through life an empty shell.

I also feel a heavy guilt of last year when I realized our daughters realized their dad might not be with us this Christmas. Yet in spite of all the deepening signs of his illness, I refused to even consider he would not be with me this year. As the next months passed I kept hope alive—even at the end, believing the start of chemo treatments would buy time. Three weeks passed with hospice care, then the last evening not even a good-bye. I was so sure of one more dawn, I left the room, what was I thinking? More dawns for me but no more for the one I loved.

The upside—our daughter and her family are in Green Valley and our great granddaughter will join us after Christmas. This week Barbara is helping me plan an open house for many friends. I could not do this without her. Ned would be so proud of us and I am moving ahead preparing to welcome our friends. Later I will put up the tree, and will remember each ornament has a special story and remembrance. My private tears will numb the pain, and I face the New Year surrounded by his gift to me—our daughter.

I'm writing, don't know what else to do.

Barbara and Dennis and our neighbors are coming for dinner tonight. It's my first formal dinner party. The holiday lights are up, table set, and I've checked to make sure I didn't forget anything. I can remember Ned always helped by making sure I didn't forget anything. He always prepared the meat on the grill. Tonight Dennis will grill the brats.

As soon as I awoke his name was on my lips. I hurried and ran the sweeper, washed the windows of the patio doors, and made a list of last-minute things to get for dinner. Then I went to the cemetery. My whole self is in mourning. Today it has been eight months since he passed away. It seemed like yesterday at the hospice home. I thought he was sleeping—I remember his beautiful white hair on the pillow; I was so careful not to wake him as I believed he needed his rest. I left the room and he was gone.

Here I am at the cemetery. I came because I wanted to be near—I cannot bring him home, I cannot feel his presence. I think it must be there is nothing left in my heart but emptiness. I will cry till there are no tears left.

It is afternoon. In two hours my guests will arrive. I will be a good hostess. There will be five of us. At his end of the table I have arranged the decorations. The table looks balanced. I will try and not see the empty place where he should sit. But it will be on my mind. Tonight will be a success because he would have wanted that.

I keep moving forward, keeping the traditions, wrapping presents, seeing friends, and it is easier to hide the pain in my heart. I only do what I have to do, what he would have wanted; sometimes I want so much to give up, but I have committed myself to the living. I will keep that promise.

Christmas

Lights
Lights of hope
In a dark night.

Christmas cards
Commercial?
I think not.
They bring connections
Welcome messages in the mailbox.
Like doves of peace
They bring a message
An affirmation of caring.
Friends shared their families,
Their journeys through the year.
This year many remembered Ned.
I too remember—and cry.

I look blankly into space,
I listen for footsteps
That will never come.
I placed an angel on the tree—
Our first angel
Fifty-seven years ago.
She has survived all the years.
I brought Christmas in our house
In memory of Ned.

I've resumed a normal life,
I do normal things.
Shop, entertain,

Wrap packages,
Attended a church service,
Remembered others.

Christmas will pass.
Christmas—then the New Year

Christmas

Christmas morning came.
Still dark December.
Awake
I pulled the blanket over my head.
I will sleep—
I will skip Christmas!

As each month passes
Seasons come and go.
Birth-death
Light-darkness
Happiness-sadness
Peace-violence.
The scales are tipped
Not balanced.

My feet hit the floor
Christmas day.
I will give
I will receive
I will be surrounded
By family/love
And I will mourn
Love lost.

New Year

New day.
New beginnings
Journeys to conqueror
Not much will change.
Rains will kiss earth
Earth will awaken.
The sleep of winter
Will soon be over.
New life will emerge
All living creatures
Will celebrate life's cycle.

Parties around the world
Celebrate happiness.
Yet violence and death
Continue the cycle.
Violence—death
God here
God there
Or nowhere?
Public journeys
Private journeys.
Celebrate the New Year
Some wish me a Happy New Year.
As I end this year
I face the new year
The rest of my life.
I can't turn back time
My heart has cried.
I don't want the new year

And all the years to come.
Around the world
People celebrate hope,
Celebrate love,
Yet hope, peace
Is like a candle
Giving beauty for only
A brief moment in time—
Yet burns out
And darkness remains.

Depression

Staring into space
Brain-dead.
No thoughts
No stimuli
No excuses
No focus
No need,
Just a glob on the couch.
No pain of loss
No desire to connect.

A few hours lost
A minute in time.
No wish to connect
Can't see the beauty
Can't remember progress
Don't want to remember holidays.

Depression arrives unannounced
A stranger at the door.
The door opens
The thief rushes in
Takes command
Of every thought,
Numbs reason.
It's like a fog
Dense—but when it leaves
It leaves victims in its path.

Ned

I want to remember
You in your chair.
Remember your voice
Remember your love.

Remembering is painful
Remembering keeps you alive in my thoughts.

Remembering is not reality.
Reality is hollow,
No laughter,
No sharing
No footsteps
No glass of milk
No goodnight.

Today I found his sleeping pills
A temptation.
It is the new year,
I've made promises
To myself and family.
I can't bring pain to family
Or to those who have given me love.

I walked into the bedroom.
The bedroom
Is a sacred place.
His/hers
Ours.
His closet
Holds his personal things.
Drivers license
Keys, billfold.
Personal clothing.
He had his privacy
He had his space.
I violated that space.
I held his billfold close to my heart,
I never touched his personal space
Now I want to touch
To hold
To try and feel his presence.
We never had twin beds
All our lives
We said "goodnight"
And knew our loved one
Was by our side.

Clothes hang limply
I hug them
I want so much to feel his presence.
His shoes
His hats
His ties.

They will go—
I am not ready.
When will I be ready
I don't know.
I will continue to read *Seven Choices*.
It helps me to know what others have experienced
The painful process of mourning.
I am selfish
I had almost fifty-seven years
Yet I wanted more.
I always believed there would be tomorrow.

Passages

These last nine months of my life have been *passages*.

Passage—the dictionary defines, 1 process of passing 2 means of passing

3 voyage 4 right of passage

For me *voyage* fits.

Last week I completed an abstract painting (it almost painted itself) and immediately I named it *Passages*.

For me painting has been a passage. It numbed my pain and gave me focus.

These months of grieving have been a passage. I've passed through deep depression, confusion, loneliness, wrong turns on my journey, and passed from dependency to confidence, and last of all passed through special events intact.

Yet I know my passage in life is not over. There are many miles to go, emotionally and physically. There are barriers to overcome, and it is not without some fears.

Passages can become like a meandering river searching to return to the sea. I do not know if I will get lost searching for who I am, what I am, or why I am. All I know is, I want my passage in life to have some meaning, purpose, and worth. Others have given freely of their time, love, and support, but

I alone have to "pass" from one mountain or valley to the next.

Passages—moving ahead, yet at each stage a look backward to remember, cherish, and embrace love lost.

Sun, rain, earth
Life, death
Each gives
Each takes away.
All whirl in an
Eternal dance.

All I ask is not to forget
Not to lament,
Not to expose my pain.

All I ask is to remember
Life's gifts.
Remember love
Remember I am not alone,
Remember to give thanks,
Remember to give back
All that life has given me.

This first year will melt into many years.
The loneliness, the pain, love lost
Will always be reality.
This first year has made me compassionate,
Wiser, stronger, and committed
To living each day left to me.

Good morning
Goodnight.
Good morning
Goodnight.

Silence
Silence

I miss
Your footsteps,
Your voice,
Your smile,
Fixing your oatmeal,
Your arms around me.

In the night
You called "Louise"
You needed me,
I was there for you.

In the end I deserted you.
I did not say good-bye.

Do you know
How much I love you?
Do you know my pain?
We had a password,
We would connect
We believed.

I'm spiritually dead.
My shadow is the real me.
My shadow walks alone.
I walk alone.

Silence
Silence

Goodnight

On My Patio

Spring has arrived.
The beauty and fury of winter has passed.
Snow fell on desert plants,
Snow laid like icing on mountaintops
Now is promise of continuation
New signs of life,
Daffodils in bloom,
Bird on pyracantha calling for a mate,
Pink on mountains
Grapefruit hang heavy on tree,
The last the sweetest of all.

A year ago a great grandchild waited patiently
For her great grandfather to help her
Pluck a grapefruit for morning breakfast.
A year ago his gentle voice gave us comfort,
His courageous journey was almost over,
He fought so hard to live.

Now that voice is silent.
He is only present in my memory.

Life's cycle continues,
The sun sets,
The moon arises,
The shadow is mine.

Shakespeare wrote of the seven stages of man,
He did not address the pain
Of those left behind.

Each evening silence
No last goodnight,
Another dawn alone.

Time passes
Streams trickle
To become dry arroyos
Until the rains return.
Earth laid bare
Ready to receive
Seeds of life.
The earth prepares
To emerge in her
Green wedding dress.

Tears like streams
Trickle into dry arroyos
Of the heart.
Empty heart,
Turned to stone.
No fertile ground
For hope to rise.

Endings and beginnings.
From birth life progresses in stages.
For every beginning there is an ending.
Some beginnings are cut short
With sudden endings.
Some endings are welcomed.

Doors are closed
And new beginnings
Offer opportunities.
If life is long
The process of closing
And opening doors,
Endings and beginnings
Are exciting.

Now I face an ending.
I reflect on the closing door.
This first year of my life
Has passed since the dearest
One in my life left this earth.
I survived this year
I survived this ending.

Beginning
The expectations for new beginnings
Feel hollow, false.
I mark the year as an ending
There is no thrill
Opening new doors.

It's no longer exciting,
I fear walking
Life alone without love.

I am a gypsy
I am going to make sentimental journeys
Europe and Asia
To visit dear families we knew.
Later I may plan to fill in
With trips to Africa, China
And wherever money and airplanes may carry me.

Maybe this is healing.
I hope to make new friends
And open my heart to those
I meet on my journeys.

For this day, April 6th
A door closed a year ago.
Memory is so painful
I think I can't survive
This day.

I need to remember the years
I was blessed with a dear husband
Who gave me love,
Confidence,
And walked this life with me.

Endings and beginnings.

I want so much to bring you home.
Many times I was lonely
When you were in the hospital,
But I knew tomorrow
You would be released.
I counted on tomorrow
Knowing I would bring you home.

Now tomorrow is here,
Reality sets in.
I know I can't bring you home,
But my heart keeps crying,
I want to bring you home
Bring you home
Bring you home.
My heart finds facing reality so painful.

Hollyhocks on the Garden Wall

On Park Bench in Bergen, Norway

I watch the world go by.
Water fountain, kids test water.
Couples share—some embrace.
Youth hurrying to somewhere.

I remember when I was
Part of a couple—alive.
Life was perfect.
I didn't always realize
Those days would pass.

Alone I wish for a sign,
Just any sign.
A dropped feather,
A voice to call my name.
I've read too many books.
I only ask to know
To understand
To accept.
I only want to know,
To believe
He is by my side.
I only ask to believe
What I cannot know.
Alone, silent, afraid.

Seagulls.
Pigeons, little sparrows
Water fountain

Children chasing birds.
Couples, families.
Sunshine like hope
Pours down on earth.
Houses, row on row
Hang on mountainside.
Fresh green leaves
Usher in spring.
Walkers stroll by.
No time or place
For tears.
Only time to love life's gifts.
Only time to remember
I once had a gift of love.

Cold beauty
Cold heart.
Look on waterfalls,
Sleek walls of rock.
Homes nestled
In mountain valleys.
Children running
To catch the train.
Friendly people,
Couples sharing.
Still cold my heart. My soul is dead.
My eyes are my camera
To capture this day.

My eyes are dams
That keep the floods behind.
I celebrate the most
Magical moment of my life—
Alone.
I celebrate for both of us.
Spring in Norway.

Fifty-eighth anniversary

On a Bus

On a bus—a vacant seat.
I fantasize
Waiting for the bus to leave.
Man walking towards the bus.
"Hurry! You'll miss the bus!"
But it's not you.
Only a wish—
The seat beside me
Remains empty.

The bus leaves.
The seat empty
As is my heart,
An empty space.

Another Bus

On bus
There's an empty seat
"Hold the bus,
He will come."
The bus moves on
The seat is still empty.
He cannot come.

I leave without him.

Train

There is a rhythm
Train moving towards its
destiny.
Fresh washed valleys,
Stream-washed walls of slate.
All pass by.
Moving,
Urgent
Click the camera,
Too slow—blur.
The moment freezes.
Life begins slow,
Gathers speed,
Breaks into a rhythm,
Days blur into months,
Months into years.

Life rushes toward its destiny.
Fortunate are those
Who get off the train occasionally,
Break the rhythm.
Open eyes and hearts to love.
Choose a different train.

Still life's rhythm
Resumes the rush toward destiny.
At last the train stops.
Alone, afraid,

A last goodbye,
One last cry
"Will no one meet me there?"

Hotel in Bergen, Norway

Cold and rainy today.
My hotel room is comfortable.
Clean, single bed.
Tears wash my face.
I gaze at a photo of Ned,
Loneliness sweeps over me.

I remember that last night,
Remember part of me died that night.
I remember a beautiful box
That held the ashes.
I want to block memory
Not to forget the one I love,
But forget the little box
Lying in desert earth.
Forget that terrible night,
Forget my failure to enfold in my arms
The last moments of his life.

I look at the bare white wall,
I stare—what do I want?
Relief from my agony.
I will sleep
Tomorrow dawn will come.
I will be OK.
I will explore, I will be thrilled
By new sights.
I will find my way
In a beautiful city.
For a few hours

I will be normal,
Able to function,
I will find my way alone

Morning—Hotel

I cried myself to sleep. Being alone in a hotel room is so painful. A stark reminder of all the hotel rooms around the world with Ned. A time to rest, share the day, plan for tomorrow, laughter, dropping into sleep with a goodnight kiss—safe, happy.

I woke this morning to gray skies. Heart breaking. Went to breakfast—so terribly lonely. The gray skies match my mood.

Yet I had one positive thought. "I might as well cry here as at home." I am glad I am making this trip. It is my sentimental journey to reconnect with those friends Ned and I care about.

I am waiting for the day to start.
My thoughts are in the blender.
Fragments of memories
Are whipped together.
I try to keep focused.
Today I will have no time for remembering,
But in this moment
I think of going home—
Opening the door.
I already felt the silence.
I think of a beautiful box
That contains ashes,
I will redirect my thoughts.

Yesterday I walked along the water's edge
At Baltic Sea.
I remembered in the past Ned and I
Walked along the edge of sand
And I gathered the lovely stones
Carved by the sea.
I picked up one of the stones
Carved by the sea—
I remembered
A remembrance service
For the departed at the church.
I remembered we were
Given a stone to hold.
What did it mean then?
I only know I kept it.

Here at the sea I held a stone,

It was the nearest to a spiritual
Experience I have ever had.
I began to gather the rocks
With love for those who may

Need a stone to hold.
I will take them home
To be given as a gift of love
To others who have lost
loved ones.

Rocks carry memories of the sea.
As do we
Carry memories etched in our
Hearts.

Germany

The sun arrives
Earth's tears are no more.
Dark fearful thoughts
Fly from me.
The village charm
Surrounds me.

Above the cobblestones,
Above the village
Stands tall the steeple,
Points to heaven—
I do not know,
But lifts,
Brings positive thoughts,
Like climbing a tower
To look below.

Standing in the tower
Is not reality.
Reality is earth,
People, love,
Above all
Love gives hope.
There is an urgency
To return one more time
To earth.
An urgency to embrace
Love one more time
Before darkness.

Damme, Germany

Hollyhocks outside my window,
Tall, confident,
Some like cups hold raindrops.
Orange daylilies
Flash their colors against a gray sky.

Grandma Netherton had hollyhocks
Along the storage wall.
They looked like patch quilts
That Grandma quilted.
Also daylilies competed for attention,
Dressed in brightest colors.

So many miles away,
So many memories,
So many years—
Granny shelling peas,
Children running in and out,
Grandkids' dogs right behind the kids!

All fades away,
The flowers die,
Loved ones are gone.
The years passed.

Other hollyhocks and daylilies bloom
In another land.
Life is renewed.

Close my eyes, drift, dream,
Floating debris parade across my dream.
Disjointed, faces I can't remember
Who, or where they crossed my path.
Lives pass through, the dream a blender.
Awake the dream vanishes,
Leaving no imprints on memory.

Do those we love
Who are no longer
Do they remember past love,
Friends, experiences?
Do they remember us?
Do our cries echo in their world?
In their spirit world do they know
We cry for them?
Or does this hope only
Exist in our dreams,
In our longings to hold love again?

So many things remind me of death.

Sea shells, white
Cold, ghostly white.
Blossoms fallen on cobblestones
Give up their beauty,
Shrivel to oblivion.
All around me
Life waiting to die.

I too wait my turn

A blank sheet of paper.
A white canvas.
A sky absent of clouds.
Fields laid bare
Not yet planted.
I am thinking
But thoughts are scrambled.
No clear visions
Past, future, now.
Blank sheet
No tears, no thoughts,
No feeling, nothing.
Nothing comes into focus.
No excitement to live,
So tempting to become
Nonexistent.

I can only try to remember
The warmth of his embrace,
To remember his comforting voice.
I try to remember what has vanished.
I look for an open door,
Sound of footsteps,
Water running in the shower,
Remember the planting,
Remember the life that has passed.

Memory is like sifting sand between my fingers.
Again cold dead thoughts, a blank sheet
A longing to be no more.

The loss seems too great to endure.

I was alone today watching
The dark waters of the Seine flow by.
I fought the urge to join
The river on its journey to the sea.
My thoughts were a cocktail

Of longing, hope, despair,
Darkness, nothing.

Travels through France

Country passes by,
Road winds around
The hills and forests
Like a gigantic snake
Curls around the Earth
And carries us on its back.

Fields of wheat
Waiting for the sun to dry.
Contented cattle
Dot the landscape.
Little villages pop up
Like magic,
Dominated by
The steeple cross,
Blessed by Pope/God.
Churchyards filled
With cold gray stones
And silent spirits.

We continue to travel
On the serpent's back.

France—a chateau that was converted in the 1400s to a hospital for the poor.

I was supposed to join a tour but was late and the tour had started; besides, the tour was in French, so I used the time to look around on my own.

On one of the large walls was a tapestry of Judgment Day. As usual in that period the sculptures, paintings, and tapestries depicted their versions of the Bible. I found myself glued to this depiction of Judgment Day. So depressing. Christ, angels, God, dead being called from their graves—some directed to go to the stairs leading to paradise, and the others, doomed, were being directed to the flames of eternal hell.

I am no longer a child but I remembered as a child the illustration of Noah and the ark; with drowning souls, Noah was safe in the ark. I felt a revolting fear, a nightmare experience of the concepts of God man has created through the ages—songs, art, stories, legends in all cultures. Still today mankind is lost in a tangle of beliefs, commitments to bring infidels to God's throne. What a waste of humanity.

I couldn't wait to leave the chateau.

Being alone in a crowded room—
The buzz of conversation,
Alive, rise and fall of volume,
People sharing,
Laughing,
Information flowing.

Being solo
Is unfamiliar
Even in a crowded room.
Pain of aloneness
Sweeps through my body.

I am here,
Yet not here.

Today was Veterans Day.
Tomorrow the American Legion
Will hold a ceremony
At the Memorial Gardens.

There lies my love
A veteran.
I will go.

There is another veteran
Of the Korean War
By his place in the cemetery.
I am thankful
The other veteran is nearby.
I think his relatives are not close
So I make sure that two flags
Commemorate this sacred place in earth.

There is a young palo verde tree
That will give shade from scorching summer sun.
There is a bench for meditation
That another loved one placed nearby.
A community of love, caring,
And remembrance.

I realize grief will never end—
Remembrance, caring, and love
Just knowing we are not alone
In life and death
Helps.

Did you know
The sun rose
As usual?
Clouds were a veil
Protecting Earth.

Did you know
It is Veterans Day
Across our nation?
America remembered,
Remembered heroes past
And those who serve today.

Do you know I remembered,
Remembered to fly the colors?
Remembered to bring a gift
Roses grown in our garden?
Do you know I was there?
Do you know I remembered?

Now the sun sets
Earth turns
Darkness falls.

I feel the dark night
Inside my heart.
Clouds of doubt and fear
Obscure the light of hope.
Cold-dark-silent thief
Steals hope.

Tomorrow is a new day to remember,
Another chance for forgiveness.
One more day to remember
Love lost.

A year and seven months,
I can't wear my grief
In a colored ribbon forever.
Move on.

My pain is like a cancer,
In spite of therapy
It grows,
Consumes my life.
The stillness gets more still,
Happy memories take a back stage
While guilt memories are more intense.
Guilt of failure
Keeps digging deeper in my soul.

My grief
Is like the Santa Cruz river.
Some places it goes underground
Only to surface at another place and time.
Grief remains a river
Flowing in my veins—a dry desert river,
But flows with intensity
When the rains come.

The only salvation for my grief
Is to be aware of others' grief,
To understand the journey
That they travel,

And in some small way
Provide a bridge
To help them cross the river.

Time

Time heals—
How much time?
How many moons
Till the tears cease?
How much time,
How much pain?
How many dawns
Will come and go?
How many nights
Will I mourn my love?
How much time to heal
A broken heart?

How much time?
How many moons will pass?

Velvet Evening

Velvet evening
Moody clouds
Obstructing moon.

Moon casts light
On drifting clouds.
White clouds
Appear like a stairway
To heaven.
Ghostly abstract
Changes as I watch.

I wonder
If all my wishes
Are like clouds
That drift away
And darkness remains.

People passing through
Some pause, some rushing
As if to catch the future.
They rush, it's their nature
As children they ran
To catch the wind,
They raced the ice flow
On river's current,
Ran, hoping to disappear
Into time—always rushing
To explore, or run away from self.

No reason except to
Catch up with life.
Each passing moment
Becomes yesterday—
But they can't know that.

They exist in now—
Making history.
Today passes so quickly
The feel of today
The warmth, the sounds,
The taste that warms the spirit.
Today becomes yesterday.

People passing through.

They don't see the red lights,
They are on green.

Do they know,
Do they experience *today*?
Is there time,
Time to love,
Time to share, time to live?

Too Soon

A time to die
Is not April.

Not when Earth awakens
From winter's sleep.

Chatter of the quail,
Snow melt on mountain,
Sleeping seeds awaken,
Rain, wind, kites,
Nest building.

Contracts with tomorrow
Starting over.

Do not leave
Stay—a bit longer
To smell the perfume
In the breeze
Feel the kiss of spring.

April
Is not a time to die.

Printed in the United States
117979LV00002B/169-186/P